Creation Write

with David Boyce

AF417924

Title:

<u>I heard some talking in the kitchen</u>

Title: _______________________________

The diner had a barrel

Title: _______________________________________

I decided to turn on the T.V.

____

____

____

____

____

____

____

____

____

____

____

____

____

____

Title: ______________________________

<u>One early morning</u> _______________________________

____

____

____

____

____

____

____

____

____

____

____

____

____

____

____

____

____

Title: ___________________________________

There was no one in the room

Title: ___________________________________

It was a difficult season for the creatures _______________________

Title: ___________________________________

It was year 2060 ____

Title: _______________________________

<u>In the region of South Africa</u>

____

____

____

____

____

____

____

____

____

____

____

____

____

____

____

Title: ______________________________

<u>I turned around</u>

Title: __________________________________

We were all excited to see __________________________________

Title: _______________________________

<u>It was a long journey</u> _______________________________

____

____

____

____

____

____

____

____

____

____

____

____

____

____

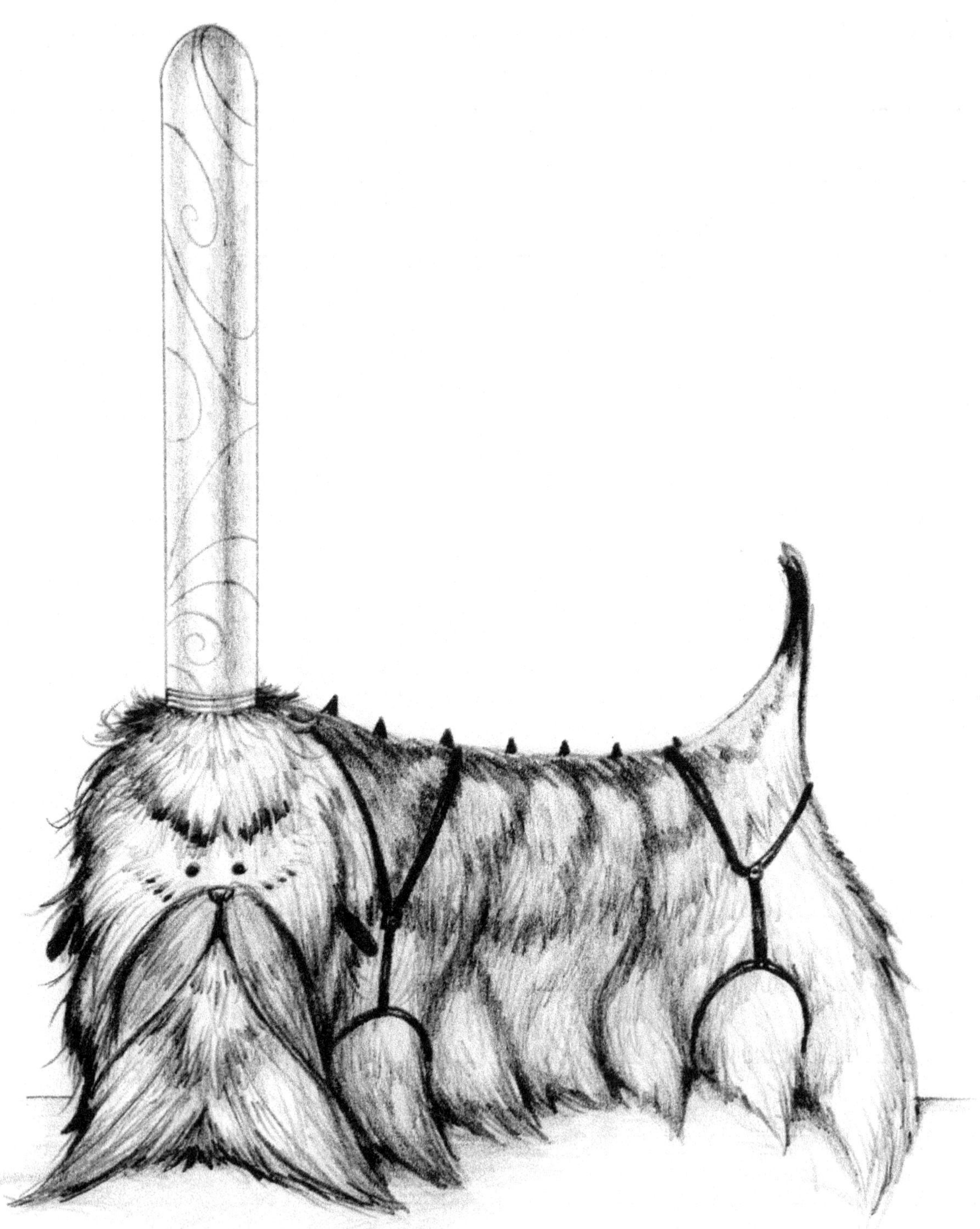

Title: ______________________________

<u>Right in front of me it happened,</u> ______________________________

____

____

____

____

____

____

____

____

____

____

____

____

____

____

Title: _______________________________________

<u>The light drops of rain had stopped</u>

Title: _______________________________

<u>The earlier nomads were known to</u> _______________________________

____

____

____

____

____

____

____

____

____

____

____

____

____

Title: _______________________________

<u>There was a set of instructions</u>

Title: ___________________________________

My eyes opened and in front of me ___________________________________

____

____

____

____

____

____

____

____

____

____

____

____

____

____

Title:

Red, purple and blue